The life we live is an encouragement itself. Document your Experiences, Testimonies and Success Stories as encouragement for your family or donate your book back to us. Your book will then be added to the Big Book of Encouragement Library as a reference for future generations.

How do you keep from getting out of character and staying true to yourself?

_____

_____

_____

_____

_____

_____

_____

_____

_____

_____

_____

_____

_____

_____

_____

_____

Bloom where you are planted

What strategies do you use to build self-confidence and self-esteem when you are feeling the most vulnerable or uncertain?

_____

_____

_____

_____

_____

_____

_____

_____

_____

_____

_____

_____

_____

_____

_____

_____

TRUST THE PROCESS

What have been some of the biggest challenges you've faced, and how did you overcome them?

_____

_____

_____

_____

_____

_____

_____

_____

_____

_____

_____

_____

_____

_____

A Mirror shows a Reflection

while

A Shadow show a Greater Version of self

How have you been able to use the challenges in your life as opportunities to grow and develop?

_____

_____

_____

_____

_____

_____

_____

_____

_____

_____

_____

_____

_____

_____

_____

@IAmEncouragement

FOCUS ON THE PROMISE
NOT WHAT'S HAPPENING

The life we live is an encouragement itself. This section is for reflection, for we cannot fix anyone other than ourselves.
Turning our Problems into Power.

Next time when challenged I pray to Recognize...

_____

_____

_____

_____

_____

_____

_____

_____

_____

_____

_____

_____

_____

_____

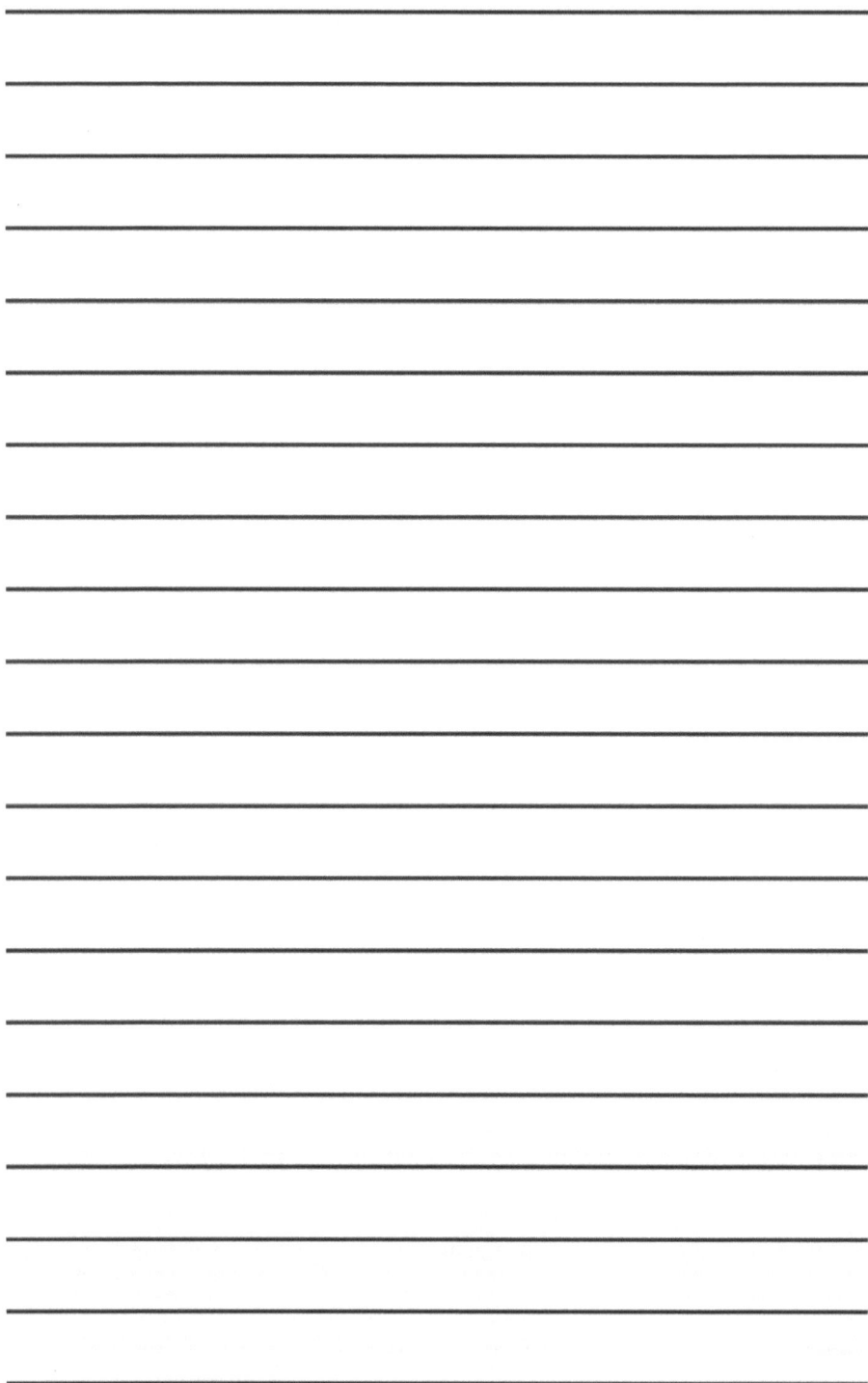

"A tree that's planted by the water isn't fazed by the fire."

I pray to be sensitive to...

WHAT WE GO THROUGH DOESN'T COMPARE TO THE BLESSINGS AFTERWARDS

@IAMENCOURAGEMENT

I pray for the ability to ...

CHOOSING IS A GESTURE OF
Free Will

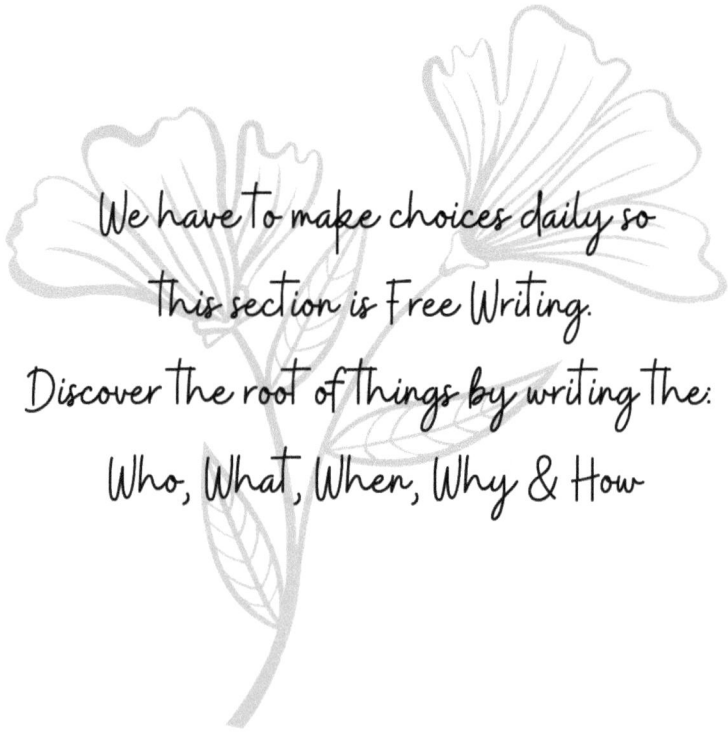

We have to make choices daily so
This section is Free Writing.
Discover the root of things by writing the:
Who, What, When, Why & How

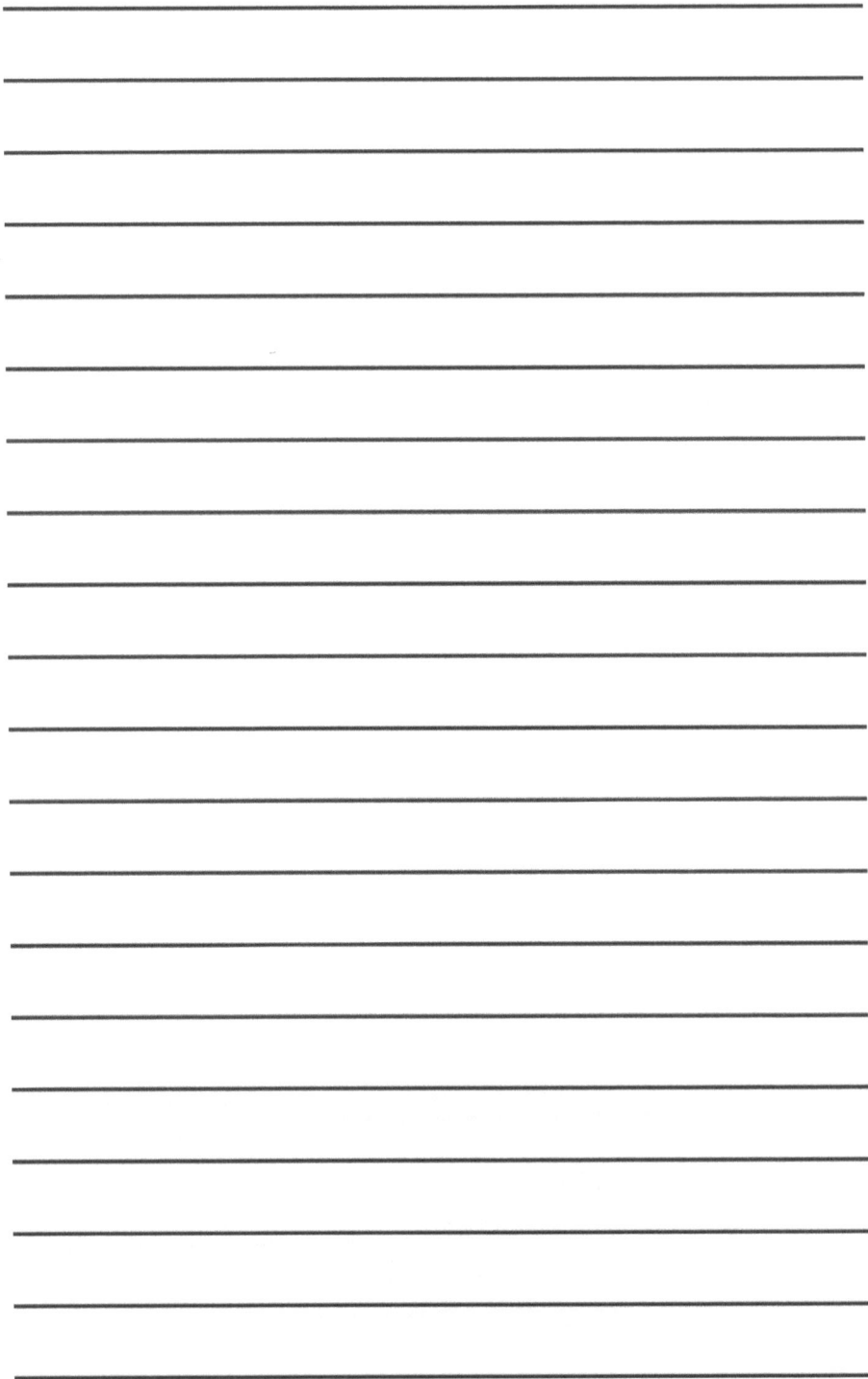

www.ingramcontent.com/pod-product-compliance
Lightning Source LLC
Chambersburg PA
CBHW040938030426
42335CB00006B/193